MW00761520

80MG
THE STORY OF AN ADDICT

Joe Osborne

www.dizzyemupublishing.com

DIZZY EMU PUBLISHING

1714 N McCadden Place, Hollywood, Los Angeles 90028

www.dizzyemupublishing.com

8OMG – The Story of an Addict

Joe Osborne

ISBN-13: 978-1537529554

First published in the United States

in 2016 by Dizzy Emu Publishing

Copyright © Joe Osborne 2016

Joe Osborne has asserted his right under the
Copyright, Designs and Patents Act 1988 to be
identified as the author of this work.

This book is sold subject to the condition that it
shall not, by way of trade or otherwise, be lent,
resold, hired out, or otherwise circulated without the
publisher's prior consent in any form of binding or
cover other than that in which it is published and
without a similar condition, including this condition,
being imposed on the subsequent purchaser.

www.dizzyemupublishing.com

EXT PARK DAY

Kevin is sitting on a bench near the waters edge.

People are playing Frisbee.

A woman walks a baby by in a stroller.

There is a homeless man under a tree sleeping.

Kevin is just watching the park.

Some Teens start messing with the homeless man, poking him.

                    KEVIN
          Hey leave him alone.

The kids scatter laughing as they run away.

The homeless man fixes his newspaper blanket and cardboard
box.

Kevin and the homeless man look at each other.

The homeless man gives him a smile and a nod

The homeless man sits up and Kevin looks away.

                    KEVIN
               (voice over)
          Today's society, a generation that
          looks down on those less fortunate
          then them as if somehow they are
          less than human.

It's fall Kevin lets out a breath that he can see as he
looks out over the water from the pond.

Kevin removes a piece of paper from his coat pocket and
unfolds it.

                    KEVIN
               (voice over)
          If they stopped and lived just a
          fragment of a mile in that persons
          shoes, would they be ashamed by
          their actions?

Kevin shakes his head and rests the paper on his leg.

A woman sits next to him on the bench.

Kevin does not notice the woman who appears to be reading a
book.

                                        (CONTINUED)

                    KEVIN
          I wish they understood, I wish
          those pampered little shits could
          see that he's a person

Kevin sighs and begins to remember.

2   INT. SIMON'S HOUSE MORNING

The camera is in really close on Simon's face.

                    KEVIN
          Still have to get it in focus, can
          you give me a sound check.

The camera zooms out and focuses

                    SIMON
          What do you want me to say?

                    KEVIN
          Good just needs a little more and
          there.

Simon blinks and sniffles.

                    KEVIN
          Ready to begin?

Simon kinda looks from side to side.

                    SIMON
          Yeah, sure I guess.

                    KEVIN
          Great, let's start with your name?

                    SIMON
          Alright, Hi my name is Simon Baker

                    KEVIN
          How old are you Simon

                    SIMON
          I am 24

                    KEVIN
          Are you an Addict?

Simon pauses for a minute and glances away then back.

                              SIMON
                    Some people think so.

                              KEVIN
                    And what do you think?

                              SIMON
                    I say I am a narcotic Enthusiast.

Simon laughs then sniffles.

                              KEVIN
                    What kind of drugs do you take?

                              SIMON
                    80's, and blues.

Simon straightens up like a reporter.

                              SIMON
                    I mean the scientific term is
                    Oxycontin or Percocets

Simon loosens back up and clears his nose.

                              SIMON
                    Sorry, this is just a little weird
                    being in front of the camera.

                              KEVIN
                    I know it can be strange, just try
                    and look past the camera at me like
                    we are just hanging out.

                              SIMON
                    What is this for again? School or
                    something?

                              KEVIN
                    I'm making a Documentary for my
                    internship, I want to be in film.

                              SIMON
                    Ah, like porn?

Kevin laughs

                              KEVIN
                    No, not porn.

                              SIMON
                    Shit man that's where the money is
                    at, you look like you could be a
                    fluffer.

                                              (CONTINUED)

                    KEVIN
          Say can I ask you something?

                    SIMON
          No I'm not taking off my pants.

                    KEVIN
          No, why do you keep sniffling.

                    SIMON
          It's kind of a habit, making sure
          it is clear.

                    JORDAN
          It's the anticipation too, see it's
          payday.

Kevin turns around as Simon's brother enters the room and
sits at the computer desk.

                    SIMON
          Yup and the mailman is taking his
          sweet ass time.

                    KEVIN
          You have a job?

                    SIMON
          No not anymore.

                    JORDAN
          He gets an unemployment check on
          Wednesday.

                    KEVIN
          How much is that?

                    SIMON
          Just enough for what I need to do.

                    KEVIN
          Then what? How do you find the
          pills?

                    SIMON
          I already made a call, it is easy
          to find around here.

A car pulls up outside the house.

                    SIMON
          Yes! finally, let me borrow your
          car Jordan.

                    JORDAN
          What if I said no?

                    SIMON
          Then I'll take it anyway, come on
          this guy is waiting just give me
          the keys.

                    JORDAN
          Fine whatever.

Jordan hands Simon the keys.

Simon runs out to the mailbox and gets in the car.

EXT SIMON'S PORCH DAY

Kevin stands on the porch for some air.

Jordan joins him outside.

Simon speeds off down the road.

Kevin leans against the railing looking around at the
street.

                    KEVIN
          So you must be his brother.

Jordan takes a joint out and sparks it up.

Jordan takes a puff and offers it to Kevin.

                    KEVIN
          No thank you I don't really smoke
          pot.

'Jordan shrugs and exhales the smoke.

                    JORDAN
          Stick around here a while you will
          change your mind.

                    KEVIN
          Must be tough for you.

                    JORDAN
          It was at first.

                    KEVIN
          And now?

Jordan takes another puff from his joint.

                                        (CONTINUED)

Jordan exhales and looks up at Kevin

                    JORDAN
          Now, well now it's just another
          day.

                    KEVIN
          I'm sorry.

Jordan laughs.

                    JORDAN
          People always say that.

                    KEVIN
          You just have to have a little
          faith.

                    JORDAN
          Faith? For what?

                    KEVIN
          That it will all turn out alright.

                    JORDAN
          Ha, you mean like everything
          happens for a reason? Like faith in
          god?

                    KEVIN
          You don't believe?

                    JORDAN
          Let me tell you a story.

Jordan takes one last puff and puts the joint out.

                    JORDAN
          To answer your question, I did
          believe, we grew up going to
          catholic school and Sunday church.

                    KEVIN
          Really?

                    JORDAN
          Yeah I know it doesn't seem like
          it, we stopped going when we moved
          here. Anyway I met a friend who
          convinced me to come to this youth
          group meeting.

                          KEVIN
                Christian?

                          JORDAN
                Yeah my mom wasn't pleased but I
                digress there was one night that I
                had been having a really rough day
                and I sent out a prayer for my
                brother.

                          KEVIN
                Was he doing drugs at that time?

                          JORDAN
                Yeah, but I didn't realize how bad
                it was. So I prayed for him to get
                better, for everything to get
                better.

                          KEVIN
                Did it help?

                          JORDAN
                After I prayed I had this
                horrendous feeling that I couldn't
                shake and that's when my mom
                called.

                          KEVIN
                What did she say?

                          JORDAN
                She said..

Jordan puts his head down.

                          JORDAN
                She said my brother was in the
                hospital with drug withdrawal.

                          KEVIN
                I'm sorry.

                          JORDAN
                That was the last time I went to
                youth group or really prayed for
                that matter.

                          KEVIN
                You lost your faith?

                    JORDAN
          Don't get me wrong I believe he's
          up there but I'm pretty sure my
          calls just go to voice mail.

                    KEVIN
          He hears you.

                    JORDAN
          Maybe, maybe not.

                    KEVIN
          Is your mom still alive?

Jordan looks away.

                    JORDAN
          Barely, not sure you could call it
          life.

Simon comes around the corner and parks quickly.

                    JORDAN
          Well he's back, you don't want to
          miss this Hollywood.

Simon gets out of the car and jumps up on the porch.

                    SIMON
          What's up fuckers.

                    JORDAN
          Just telling Spielberg here his
          money shot's coming up.

Jordan goes inside.

                    SIMON
          Smoking pot without me guy jeez.

                    JORDAN
          Figured you had your own fun.

                    SIMON
          You want one this time guy?

                    JORDAN
          I'm good.

                    SIMON
          Allright guy, you don't know what
          you're missing. How about you
          Michael Moore so i know you're not
          wearing a wire.

                              KEVIN
                    No thanks.

                              SIMON
                    No? Suit yourself more for me and
                    Debbie.

Simon walks in the house.

Kevin sits there for a second and looks down at himself.

                              KEVIN
                    Michael Moore? is that a fat joke
                    or something?

Kevin walks in the house.

INT. SIMON'S HOUSE AFTERNOON

Kevin sits on the couch and gets his camera ready.

                              KEVIN
                    So vocalize the process for me so
                    my viewers can understand step by
                    step.

                              SIMON
                    Well first things first I have to
                    clear my nasal passage.

Simon tries to clear each nostril.

Simon pours water into his nose and lets it drip into the
sink.

                              KEVIN
                    That looks uncomfortable.

                              SIMON
                    Yeah once in a while I get water
                    going the wrong way but now I know
                    I'm clear.

                              KEVIN
                    Alright so when does your
                    girlfriend get here?

Jordan laughs comfortably high in the computer chair.

                              SIMON
                    What are you talking about?

(CONTINUED)

                         JORDAN
          I believe He means Debbie.

                         KEVIN
          Is she just a friend?

                         JORDAN
          Oh no she helps a lot, in fact
          without Debbie there could be no
          fun.

                         SIMON
          You're getting too far ahead
          Spielberg.

Simon takes out the pill and his License.

Simon spits on his hand and rubs the pill between his
fingers.

                         SIMON
          I know it seems gross but it's the
          only way to get the coating off.

                         KEVIN
          You don't do the coating?

                         SIMON
          No personally I think it's a nasty
          taste.

Kevin moves from the couch closer to the table where Simon
has the pill on a clipboard.

Simon takes the pill and puts his license on top of it like
a knife and pushes down.

                         SIMON
          The key is to apply enough pressure
          to split it but not enough to send
          it flying.

Simon applies more pressure and splits it perfectly in two.

Jordan claps.

                         SIMON
          Thank you, two Perfect halves.

                         JORDAN
          An artist at work.

                         SIMON
                Next we crush it.

Simon turns the license over and applies pressure on the
first half and crushes it.

Simon cuts it up with his ID into fine powder and does the
same with the other half.

Simon cuts the fine powder into a couple different lines.

                         SIMON
                Are you ready to meet Debbie?

                         KEVIN
                Yeah.

Simon pulls out a green tube and points to the side of it
which says Debbie.

                         SIMON
                This is Debbie.

                         KEVIN
                Oh I see now, that's clever.

                         SIMON
                I thought so. Now for the fun part.

Simon covers one nostril and puts the straw in the other.

Simon leans down to the clipboard

Simon blows the first line.

Simon picks his head up exhaling and opening his eyes wide
then shutting them.

                         SIMON
                Woohoo that was a good one, now for
                round two.

Simon takes a deep breath and then clogs his nostril and
finishes off the second line.

Simon puts the straw down and puts the clipboard behind the
chair.

                         SIMON
                And now we wait.

                                        (CONTINUED)

                    KEVIN
          Wait for what?

                    SIMON
          The drip.

                    KEVIN
          Can you look in the camera and
          explain what that is?

                    SIMON
          It's when the powder moves through
          my nasal passage and drips into the
          back of my throat.

Simon sits in the chair and leans his head back really
relaxed.

                    SIMON
          Ah, there it is.

                    KEVIN
          It gets you high that fast?

                    SIMON
          Yeah, only takes a few minutes and
          comes over like a wave.

Mrs. Baker yells from down the hall

                    MRS. BAKER
          I know you guys are smoking pot in
          my house, knock it off.

                    JORDAN
          No we're not.

                    MRS. BAKER
          I can fucking smell it. don't
          fucking lie to me.

Mrs. Baker slams the bathroom door.

                    KEVIN
          Who was that?

                    SIMON
          Our mother, You should go man it
          could get real ugly.

                    KEVIN
          Why? Because of the pot?

> SIMON
> It would just be better if you
> weren't here, She's well she's a
> story for another day.

> KEVIN
> Alright fair enough, thank you for
> your time.

Kevin packs his camera gear and leaves the house.

As Kevin leaves he can hear Mrs. Bakers footsteps coming
toward the kitchen.

INT. KEVIN'S HOUSE NIGHT

Kevin sits at a computer desk with his headphones on typing
and recording the notes from the day.

Kevin's mom approaches him from behind.

Kevin keeps typing unaware his mother is behind him.

> MRS. BROOKE
> Kevin?

Mrs. Brooke reaches out and grabs Kevin's shoulder.

Kevin jumps out of his seat

Mrs. Brooke jumps.

Kevin takes his headphones off.

> KEVIN
> Wow mom you scared the crap out of
> me.

> MRS. BROOKE
> Didn't you hear me calling you?

Kevin takes a breath and starts to laugh.

> KEVIN
> No, I had my headphones in. You
> snuck right up on me like a ninja.

Mrs. Brooke and Kevin start laughing.

> MRS. BROOKE
> So what are you working on?

Kevin turns and looks at the screen then looks back at his
mother.

                              KEVIN
                    Oh it's my project for class, A
                    documentary.

Mrs. Brooke Looks over Kevin's shoulder.

                              MRS. BROOKE
                    What's it about?

                              KEVIN
                    It's a special interest piece on
                    Addiction.

                              MRS. BROOKE
                    Sounds very interesting, just
                    please be careful.

                              KEVIN
                    I will.

Kevin walks into the kitchen to fridge and grabs beer.

Mrs. Brooke starts to walk away and stops.

Kevin walks back to the computer and cracks the beer and
takes a sip.

Mrs. Brooke walks back with a concerned/sad look on her
face.

                              MRS. BROOKE
                    Kevin?

                              KEVIN
                    Yeah mom?

                              MRS. BROOKE
                    Does this have anything to do with
                    your father?

Kevin just keeps looking at the screen and typing.

                              KEVIN
                    No, why would it?

                              MRS. BROOKE
                    No reason, Dinner's in five.

Kevin puts his headphones back on and continues typing.

Mrs. Brooke walks away.

When He's sure she is gone Kevin stops typing.

Kevin brings up a picture on the computer of a teen and a father dressed in a Army uniform.

Kevin sighs and sips his beer.

Kevin closes the picture and continues typing.

INT UNIVERSITY MEDIA LAB DAY

Kevin is sitting at the computer in front of the window looking out to the grassy area.

Kevin is editing the footage He got from Simons.

Todd comes into the media lab.

Kevin turns around.

                    TODD
          Hey what's going on Kev?

                    KEVIN
          Hey Todd, Not much just rendering
          some footage I caught for my
          Documentary.

Todd slings his backpack on the floor and sits next to Kevin.

Todd takes off his sunglasses.

                    TODD
          Oh wow, who turned up the fucking
          sun. Can't I get a cloud or
          something.

Kevin laughs.

                    KEVIN
          Late night?

                    TODD
          Dude you have nooo idea.

                    KEVIN
          Do you have a clue of what your
          project is going to be?

                    TODD
          Nope, I do however know that I need
          some aspirin.

Todd puts his head on the desk.

                              KEVIN
                    What are you doing?

                              TODD
                    Waiting for inspiration to strike
                    and the Aspirin fairy to come ease
                    my pain.

Kevin reaches in his bag and takes out the bottle of
Aspirin.

Kevin tosses the bottle at Todd.

                              TODD
                    Aha my theory is correct.

                              KEVIN
                    And that would be?

                              TODD
                    Good things come to those who party
                    and then procrastinate.

Kevin laughs

Todd cracks and a water and takes the pills.

Kevin looks out into the grassy area and sees a homeless
man.

The homeless man is carrying a filthy backpack and walking
toward a shady tree.

                              TODD
                    What are you looking at space
                    cadet.

Todd looks out the window.

                              TODD
                    Oh that crazy nut?

                              KEVIN
                    What makes you think He's crazy?

                              TODD
                    He's always hanging around here and
                    I have heard him mumbling to
                    himself.

Students walk by the homeless man and He extends his hands
out for money.

The students pass him by and snicker to each other as they walk by.

The homeless man continues towards his tree mouthing something.

>   TODD
>   See what did I tell you He's
>   talking to himself right now.

>   KEVIN
>   No one stops to help him?

>   TODD
>   Are you kidding? I'm not going near
>   him.

>   KEVIN
>   He looks like a Vet.

>   TODD
>   What if it's a disguise and then
>   Bam! you wind up being taken back
>   to his place and eaten.

>   KEVIN
>   Good luck with that.

Kevin grabs his backpack.

>   TODD
>   Hey, where you going?

>   KEVIN
>   I have to go get some books from
>   the library and this footage will
>   take a while to render.

Kevin starts to walk out the door.

>   TODD
>   Hey Kev, man don't forget what I
>   said.

>   KEVIN
>   About what?

>   TODD
>   About not getting eaten by some
>   homeless dude.

Kevin shakes his head laughing and walks out of the lab.

7   INT UNIVERSITY LIBRARY DAY

Kevin is walking down the aisles looking at books.

The Librarian's assistant approaches him.

                    LIBRARY ASSISTANT
          Hi can I help you find something.

                    KEVIN
          Yeah I'm looking for anything
          having to do with Drug addiction.

                    LIBRARY ASSISTANT
          Alright let's see here.

The library assistant starts walking Kevin down the book
aisle searching.

                    LIBRARY ASSISTANT
          Ah, here we are, this is a book on
          the effects and signs of addiction.

Kevin picks up the book.

                    LIBRARY ASSISTANT
          Does that help?

                    KEVIN
          Yes, it is pretty much exactly what
          I'm looking for.

                    LIBRARY ASSISTANT
          Awesome, well let me know if
          there's anything else I can do for
          you.

The library assistant smiles and walks away.

Kevin checks her out as she walks.

                    KEVIN
          Man I love student aids.

                    CREEPY PROFESSOR
          Mm me too.

Kevin turns to see a older teacher standing there.

Kevin looks at him funny for a minute and then walks to the
table to read his book.

Kevin spends a while flipping through the book and taking
notes.

                                              (CONTINUED)

Kevin puts the book down and stretches for a minute.

Kevin glances out the window and sees the old homeless man under the tree.

The old man is warming up his hands.

The old man looks up to the sky and smiles.

Kevin throws his notebook in his bag and walks up to the library assistant to hand her the book.

>   KEVIN
>   Hi, I think I'm going to check you
>   out.

Kevin smacks his head.

The assistant cracks a smile.

>   KEVIN
>   The book, I would like to check the
>   book out is what I was trying to
>   say.

The Assistant opens the back of the book and Scans it and drops a note in the back and gives it back to Kevin.

>   KEVIN
>   Thank you.

>   LIBRARY ASSISTANT
>   You're welcome, have a great day.

Kevin walks out of the library.

INT UNIVERSITY CAFETERIA DAY

Kevin waits in line at the coffee hut

Todd walks in to the cafeteria.

>   TODD
>   Hey Kevin.

>   KEVIN
>   Hey man.

>   TODD
>   Your project finally rendered so I
>   saved it for ya, I wasn't sure when
>   you were coming back.

                         KEVIN
               Yeah, I guess I got caught up in
               the research, thank you for saving
               it though.

                         TODD
               Not a problem, I'm going off campus
               for some food, Do you wanna come?

                         KEVIN
               Thanks but I'm going to stick
               around here a bit and maybe do some
               more filming later.

                         TODD
               Alright buddy I'll catch ya later
               and hey thanks for the aspirin.

                         KEVIN
               Anytime.

Todd leaves the cafeteria.

Kevin gets to the front of the line.

Kevin makes two large coffees black.

Kevin picks up creamers and sugars and heads out the door.

9   EXT UNIVERSITY PARK DAY

The old homeless man is sitting under the tree smiling and
looking at the water.

Kevin walks up to him.

                         KEVIN
               Hey mister, would you like a hot
               coffee?

The old man looks up to Kevin.

Kevin outstretches his hand.

The old man cautiously takes the cup and smiles as he smells
it.

                         KEVIN
               I wasn't sure how you took it, if
               you need cream or sugar I have
               them.

                         JOHN
              Black is fine.

Kevin sips his coffee.

                         KEVIN
              My names Kevin.

Kevin reaches his hand out to shake John's.

John reaches out and shakes Kevin's hand.

                         JOHN
              My name's John.

                         KEVIN
              Good to meet you John, mind if I
              sit down?

                         JOHN
              No, Go ahead.

Kevin sits on the grass.

John sips his coffee and warms his hands up.

                         KEVIN
              It's a little brisk out here with
              the wind I figured you could use
              something warm.

                         JOHN
              I appreciate that, your different
              from the other students.

                         KEVIN
              How so.

John and Kevin sip their coffees.

                         JOHN
              Well, your the only one who's
              bothered to come and talk to be and
              be nice.

                         KEVIN
              It's no big deal, it's just a
              coffee.

                         JOHN
              Hey now don't sell yourself short,
              you took time out of your day to
              help a complete stranger. A little
              kindness can go a long way.

                                        (CONTINUED)

                         KEVIN
              I suppose you're right.

                         JOHN
              I like this place, looking at the
              water is calming don't you think.

                         KEVIN
              Yes, really is a peaceful place. Is
              that why you come here?

                         JOHN
              That's one reason.

Kevin sips his coffee.

                         KEVIN
              And the other?

                         JOHN
              I'm waiting.

                         KEVIN
              Waiting for what.

                         JOHN
              That is not an short easy answer.

                         KEVIN
              Were you in the military?

                         JOHN
              Yeah, that was a good while ago,
              almost seems like another life.

John peers into the water remembering his past.

                         KEVIN
              So do you have a home?

                         JOHN
              You're looking at it kid.

Kevin looks around.

                         KEVIN
              Why don't you go to a shelter.

John looks at the sky and cracks a laugh.

                         KEVIN
              I'm sorry It's none of my business.

(CONTINUED)

                              JOHN
                    It's fine, you want to know why I
                    choose here?

                              KEVIN
                    If you want to tell me.

John points to the sky.

                              JOHN
                    You can't beat the view.

Kevin looks up and then thinks about it, laughs and nods his
head.

They both laugh and drink their coffee.

                              KEVIN
                    Yeah, I think I can dig that.

                              JOHN
                    Dig?

                              KEVIN
                    Yeah, it means like understand,
                    it's what the cool kids say these
                    days.

Kevin's phone goes off.

Kevin looks at it and responds.

                              JOHN
                    Is that your old lady?

Kevin laughs and puts the phone in his pocket.

                              KEVIN
                    No, that was the talent, I actually
                    have no old lady.

                              JOHN
                    Talent?

                              KEVIN
                    Yeah, I'm a film student making a
                    documentary for my senior class.

                              JOHN
                    Interesting, What about?

                         KEVIN
              It's about drug addiction.

                         JOHN
              Wow that's a heavy subject, good
              luck on it.

                         KEVIN
              Yeah, Listen stay warm alright.

                         JOHN
              I will, and thank you for the
              coffee and the chat.

                         KEVIN
              You're welcome.

         Kevin gets up and starts to walk away.

                         JOHN
              Hey Kevin.

         Kevin turns around.

                         KEVIN
              Yeah?

                         JOHN
              Stay safe kid, It's a dangerous
              world your diving into.

                         KEVIN
              I will be.

10   INT. SIMON'S HOUSE AFTERNOON

         Kevin comes in the front door and into the living room.

                         KEVIN
              I got your message what's wrong?

         Simon's on the floor agitated and in pain.

                         SIMON
              Fucking holiday.

                         KEVIN
              What? Your text said emergency.

                         SIMON
              I need some cash, I don't get my
              check until tomorrow.

                         KEVIN
          Are you serious? that's the
          emergency?

                         SIMON
          You have no idea how bad this
          hurts.

                         JORDAN
          You said you were gonna space them
          out.

                         KEVIN
          Them?

                         JORDAN
          Yeah he got two last time. Wait no
          to be accurate I got two.

                         SIMON
          I was planning on spacing them out
          but I got done one and then just
          wanted another bump.

                         KEVIN
          How much do you need?

                         JORDAN
          Don't do it man, you will regret
          it.

                         SIMON
          Quit bitching about your money
          Jordan, not like you don't get paid
          again in a couple days.

                         JORDAN
          Not the point you fucking asshole,
          You didn't even ask. I'm trying to
          save money up and I can't do that
          when you take my whole paychecks.

                         SIMON
          At least your not the one in pain
          right now.

                         JORDAN
          Who's fault is that you idiot.

                         KEVIN
          You guys are family you shouldn't
          be acting like this, how much do
          you need.

                              SIMON
                    I can get one for 70. I'll pay you
                    back.

                              KEVIN
                    Just this one last time then you're
                    on your own.

                              SIMON
                    Thank you man, Hollywood to the
                    rescue.

Kevin reaches in his wallet and pulls out 70 dollars and
holds it in his hand.

                              KEVIN
                    I'm doing this on one condition.

                              SIMON
                    What?

                              KEVIN
                    You do it here and you stop
                    stealing money from your brother.

                              SIMON
                    Fine.

Kevin hands him the cash.

Simon sends a text and stands up.

Simon opens the blinds a little to see the road.

A car pulls to the end of the road and stops no one gets
out.

                              SIMON
                    Alright that's him I'll be right
                    back.

Simon leaves the house and walks toward the car.

Jordan and Kevin watch from the window.

                              JORDAN
                    You know He's not going to stop
                    stealing money from me.

                              KEVIN
                    I don't get why He does it, you
                    guys are family.

                                        (CONTINUED)

                    JORDAN
      We're more like a broken family,
      and you want some advice?

                    KEVIN
      Sure.

                    JORDAN
      Never trust the word of a junkie,
      They'll say anything for a fix.

                    KEVIN
      Where's your mom during all this?

                    JORDAN
      My moms gone, she has been for
      years.

                    KEVIN
      I'm confused I thought I heard her
      one day.

                    JORDAN
      That's her, I meant mentally gone.
      She just sleeps and eats and yells
      randomly.

                    KEVIN
      Do you think that's why Simon does
      this?

                    JORDAN
      I don't know, and to be honest I
      don't care. As soon as I can
      graduate I'm going to college, The
      only sane ones around here are me
      and my dad.

                    KEVIN
      Where is your father?

                    JORDAN
      My dad works a lot so we can still
      keep up with the bills since my mom
      up and quit going to work.

                    KEVIN
      That's rough, your father sounds
      like a good man.

                    JORDAN
      He really is, and as hard as he
      works my brother keeps stealing
      money from them too.

                                    (CONTINUED)

                              KEVIN
          How?

Jordan puts his head down in shame.

                              JORDAN
                    That's my guilt to bear.

Simon hands the car the money and takes a little Cellophane.

The car drives off.

Simon comes back to the house.

Simon immediately busts out the clipboard and does half of
the pill to his head.

Simon changes his shirt which is drench in sweat.

                              SIMON
                    Oh man that's better, Phew.

Simon sits down in the chair and lights a cigarette.

                              KEVIN
                    Feel better now?

                              SIMON
                    Yeah. Thank you man you're a life
                    saver?

                              JORDAN
                    Because going without for a whole
                    day would have killed you right?

                              SIMON
                         (sarcastically)
                    Yup, I'm pretty sure it would.

                              KEVIN
                    Have you ever thought of stopping.

                              SIMON
                    Why would I?

                              KEVIN
                    Aren't you tired of getting sick
                    and needing it, I mean 20 minutes
                    ago you were about pass out.

                              SIMON
                    Every high has to have a low.

                    KEVIN
          Yeah but come on man this is no way
          to live.

                    SIMON
          Would you rather I was a GSA?

                    KEVIN
          What's a GSA?

                    SIMON
          Do you drink beer?

                    KEVIN
          Yeah?

                    SIMON
          When? to celebrate, to feel good?
          When you're stressed?

                    KEVIN
          Yeah, every now and again, what's
          your point?

                    SIMON
          My point is sometimes you want that
          drink or almost need it right?

                    KEVIN
          No, I don't need it. I enjoy it.

                    SIMON
          Bam, there it is and I enjoy this.

                    KEVIN
          What bam? that's not close to the
          same thing, I have a beer or three
          a week.

                    SIMON
          It's still a habit, I started off
          with pills being able to control it
          and it slowly got worse, just like
          with an alcoholic but an alcoholic
          is Government sanctioned.

                    KEVIN
          That's some kind of logic sir.

                    SIMON
          I know it blows your mind.

                    KEVIN
          But the issue I have with your
          point is the government controls
          the FDA which makes the pills. So
          aren't you already a Government
          sanctioned Junky?

                    SIMON
          Don't call me a junky, I'm just
          aggressively recreational. Have you
          ever thought of quitting drinking?

                    KEVIN
          No because it's not a problem for
          me.

                    SIMON
          Well neither is this for me, an yet
          why can't I go to the grocery store
          and pick up a six pack of pills but
          you can buy beer. Seems unfair to
          me.

                    JORDAN
          Wow, you are truly delusional.

                    SIMON
          Well my delusions are a lot less
          fucked up then the world we
          actually live in.

Kevin checks his phone.

                    KEVIN
          Well I have to get going, as much
          fun as this has been. Can you do me
          a favor?

                    SIMON
          What's that?

                    KEVIN
          Stop asking me for money, and also
          write in this.

Kevin hands Simon a blank notebook.

                    SIMON
          What am I suppose to write?

                    KEVIN
          How you're feeling, I want you to
          describe the high and anything else
          you want to write in there.

                         SIMON
          Dude like a diary? fuck that.

                         KEVIN
          Just hang on to it, and more like a
          insider look to your mind.

                         SIMON
          Yeah whatever man anyway thanks for
          the save today I was hurting.

                         JORDAN
          Wouldn't be hurting if you just
          quit.

                         SIMON
          Man just give that up.

                         KEVIN
          Not for nothing but he has a point
          you know. Anyway I'm out of here.

Kevin leaves the house and gets in his car and drives away.

INT. KEVIN'S HOUSE NIGHT

An exhausted Kevin sits at the computer with two empty beer
bottles typing more on the report.

Mrs. Brooke walks into room.

                         MRS. BROOKE
          Hey Kevin how's the project going.

Kevin's computer freezes.

                         KEVIN
          No, what come on.

Kevin tries to get his computer back.

                         KEVIN
              Shit!

Kevin turns around.

                         KEVIN
          How's it going? Well not that well
          at the moment and it would go a
          whole lot better if you weren't
          breathing down my neck.

Mrs. Brooke takes a step back in shock.

                                              (CONTINUED)

                    MRS. BROOKE
          Well where did that come from.

                    KEVIN
          I just did a lot of work and now
          poof it probably all went away.

Kevin finishes his beer and gets up to go to the fridge.

                    MRS. BROOKE
          Are you drunk?

Kevin looks at his mom.

                    KEVIN
          Good deducing Sherlock.

                    MRS. BROOKE
          This isn't you why are you doing
          this?

                    KEVIN
          Why not I think is the better
          question, just one more beer. Have
          one with me.

                    MRS. BROOKE
          I think you've had enough for
          tonight.

                    KEVIN
          Party pooper.

Kevin stumbles back to the chair and looks at the frozen
computer.

                    MRS. BROOKE
          Kevin I think this project is
          having a negative influence on you,
          can't you choose a different
          subject?

                    KEVIN
          Nope, It's too late to go back now
          I'm already invested, literally.

                    MRS. BROOKE
          You gave money to him!

                    KEVIN
          It's cool it was a two time thing
          we have a understanding now.

(CONTINUED)

                         MRS. BROOKE
          This has to stop.

                         KEVIN
          It will, we agreed he would stop
          stealing money from his brother and
          find his own way to pay for it.

                         MRS. BROOKE
          No you have enough footage and
          notes for the project stop going to
          see him.

                         KEVIN
          Fine, whatever.

                         MRS. BROOKE
          Fine what?

                         KEVIN
          Fine I'll stop going over there.

                         MRS. BROOKE
          Thank you, I know you think you are
          helping but you're just enabling
          him, sometimes you just have to
          know when to give up.

                         KEVIN
          Like you gave up on dad.

                         MRS. BROOKE
          That's not fair I didn't give up on
          your father.

                         KEVIN
          Really then where is he huh? Why
          didn't you stop him from leaving?

                         MRS. BROOKE
          Your father gave up on himself, and
          on us. It was just better this way
          trust me.

                         KEVIN
          You should have done something!

                         MRS. BROOKE
          You don't think I tried? I tried to
          hang on but I couldn't anymore we
          just grew apart.

                                              (CONTINUED)

                              KEVIN
                    That is the lamest excuse I've
                    heard, great now I'm sober.

Kevin goes to the fridge and grabs another one.

Kevin sits back down in the chair.

                              MRS. BROOKE
                    I'm going to forgive you because
                    you're drunk and I will talk to you
                    when you're sober goodnight.

Mrs. Brooke calmly walks away.

As she turns away from Kevin she is fighting back tears.

Kevin leans back in the chair and looks outside

Kevin sips his beer and walks to the window to look at the
stars.

Kevin stares into the night sky and sighs.

Kevin looks at his beer and walks to the sink.

Kevin pours the rest of the beer down the drain.

12   INT KEVIN'S HOUSE MORNING

Mrs. Brooke walks into the kitchen.

                              MRS. BROOKE
               Kevin?

Mrs. Brooke looks around and notices the coffee is made and
there is a note.

Mrs. Brooke opens the note and reads it.

                              KEVIN
                         (Voice Over)
                    Mom, I'm sorry about last night, I
                    guess this project is bringing up
                    old memories. Anyway I figured the
                    least I could do was make coffee.
                    Left for class early, I'll be home
                    later. Love ya.

Mrs. Brooke smiles and pours a cup of coffee.

INT CAFETERIA MORNING

Kevin goes to the breakfast section and gets two sausage and cheese muffins and two coffees.

Kevin goes to the counter and swipes his student food card.

Todd walks up behind him with a coffee.

                    TODD
          Hey man.

                    KEVIN
          Hey, How's it going.

                    TODD
          Good, you?

Kevin yawns and grabs his head in pain.

                    TODD
          Man, looks like you had a rough
          night.

                    KEVIN
          Yeah it wasn't great.

                    TODD
          How's the project coming?

                    KEVIN
          I don't really know, I might scrap
          it.

                    TODD
          You're kidding.

                    KEVIN
          I have been drinking more lately
          and me and my mom got in a huge
          fight last night. I told her I
          would stop doing research on the
          addict.

                    TODD
          That's rough.

                    KEVIN
          Yeah it kind of brought up memories
          of my father.

(CONTINUED)

                    TODD
          Shit man, so you coming up to the
          studio?

                    KEVIN
          Yeah in a bit going to go have
          breakfast with John.

                    TODD
          John?

                    KEVIN
          Yeah the homeless guy that always
          sits in our park there.

                    TODD
          That's his name? is he a weirdo?

                    KEVIN
          Nah man, He's just like you and me
          and actually pretty smart.

                    TODD
          Wow, you're braver then me pal,
          I'll see ya up there.

                    KEVIN
          Yeah, if you're looking for creepy
          you should check out the professor
          that hangs out in the library.

                    TODD
          Oh? I know the student aid up there
          is smoking hot.

                    KEVIN
          Yeah, I have to go there today and
          return the book.

                    TODD
          There ya go bud, gonna hit that?

                    KEVIN
          Ha ha, I doubt that, I'll see ya up
          there.

                    TODD
          Alright, make me proud.

Kevin shakes his head and laughs then walks away.

EXT UNIVERSITY PARK DAY

Kevin walks up to John sitting on the grass in the shade of
a tree. Kevin hands him a breakfast sandwich.

>   JOHN
>   Thank you Kevin.

>   KEVIN
>   Well I figured you could use a
>   little hot food.

Kevin yawns and sits down to sip his coffee.

>   JOHN
>   You look exhausted, are you feeling
>   alright?

>   KEVIN
>   Yeah, just a long night which
>   included getting too drunk and a
>   huge fight with my mother.

>   JOHN
>   Really? you don't strike me as the
>   typical drinking student.

>   KEVIN
>   Normally I'm not but I think this
>   project has dredged up some
>   memories that aren't good ones.

>   JOHN
>   Take it from someone who has been
>   down that road, drinking will not
>   ease those bad memories.

>   KEVIN
>   Yeah I know and me and my mom
>   usually get along, it's just.. I
>   guess it doesn't matter.

>   JOHN
>   No tell me, I can be a good
>   listener.

>   KEVIN
>   We fought about my father. I feel
>   like she gave up on him.

>   JOHN
>   I'm sure it wasn't like that.

                              KEVIN
                    She just let him go, didn't try to
                    stop him.

                              JOHN
                    I'm sorry.

                              KEVIN
                    Thanks I appreciate that but He
                    should be sorry.

                              JOHN
                    Have you ever tried to track him
                    down?

                              KEVIN
                    That thought crossed my mind but I
                    don't remember much, or even his
                    name. Besides what would be the
                    point?

                              JOHN
                    Aren't you curious about him?

                              KEVIN
                    Curious about what, why he left us?
                    Why we weren't good enough for him?

          Kevin's phone goes off.

          Kevin looks at it and ignores it.

                              JOHN
                    I'm sorry I shouldn't have pried.

                              KEVIN
                    Really it's fine.

          Kevin's phone keeps going off.

                              JOHN
                    Is that you're mother that keeps
                    calling?

                              KEVIN
                    Nope, it's Simon.

                              JOHN
                    The addict?

                              KEVIN
                    Yeah, I told my mom I would be done
                    with the research.

                        JOHN
          How come?

                        KEVIN
          Well she's worried about my safety
          and how it's changing me.

                        JOHN
          Safety? did something happen?

                        KEVIN
          No, nothing bad, He's extremely
          intelligent you know? like
          manipulative, He's talked me into
          giving him money a couple times.

                        JOHN
          Addicts will say anything to get
          the next fix.

                        KEVIN
          Yeah, well I have enough research
          and I told him no more money from
          me or his brother. I kind of feel
          bad for him though.

                        JOHN
          Why's that?

                        KEVIN
          Well he's got his brother who seems
          very loyal or hopeless and He's
          broken his parent's trust, just
          seems like everyone gave up on him.
          Even I really just used him for my
          project.

                        JOHN
          There's one important thing to
          remember.

                        KEVIN
          What's that?

                        JOHN
          He's only got himself to blame.

                        KEVIN
          Yeah.. I suppose you're right, well
          I enjoyed our chat as usual but I
          have to return some books.

(CONTINUED)

                         JOHN
          Thank you for the coffee and for
          the food, you're a good man.

                         KEVIN
          See ya tomorrow.

Kevin walks away

                         JOHN
          Hey kid wait!

Kevin stops and turns

                         JOHN
          You're father would be proud of the
          man you've become.

Kevin looks at John for a moment then nods his head and
walks away.

15   INT UNIVERSITY LIBRARY DAY

Kevin walks into the library and up to the front desk with
the books.

Kevin waits for the library assistant to come to the desk.

                    LIBRARY ASSISTANT
          Find everything you need?

The assistant comes around the desk and Kevin checks her
out.

                         KEVIN
          MMhmmm.

Kevin opens his mouth in surprise for saying what he was
thinking out loud.

                         KEVIN
          I mean yes, I'd like to return
          these.

The assistant looks down and smiles and grabs the books.

                    LIBRARY ASSISTANT
          I think what you're doing is great.

                         KEVIN
          You do?

                    LIBRARY ASSISTANT
          Yeah, most people don't have the
          courage to try to better
          themselves.

Kevin looks at her confused.

                    LIBRARY ASSISTANT
          The books, I mean aren't you a.

                    KEVIN
          A what? OH, oh an addict? no these
          books aren't for me I'm doing a
          project.

                    LIBRARY ASSISTANT
          Oh god, I am so sorry.

Kevin laughs

                    LIBRARY ASSISTANT
          I am so embarrassed now.

                    KEVIN
          No, I mean do I come off as that?

                    LIBRARY ASSISTANT
          No actually I just assumed, I don't
          know.

Kevin reaches out his hand to shake hers.

                    KEVIN
          Well Allow me to introduce myself,
          I am Kevin.

The Assistant shakes his hand.

                    LIBRARY ASSISTANT
          Hi, I'm Kristen

                    KEVIN
          Well it's good to meet you.

They smile for a minute at each other.

Kristen stands up and clears her throat.

                    KRISTEN
          Well I have to go put these away
          but here.

Kristen writes her number down on a piece of paper.

                         KRISTEN
              Maybe you can text me sometime and
              we can hang out.

                         KEVIN
              I would like that.

                         KRISTEN
              Cool.

                         KEVIN
              I will definitely text you.

Kristen bumps into the desk walking away backwards.

Kristen smiles and walks away with the cart of books.

Kevin watches her leave.

                         KEVIN
              Wow that was unexpected.

                         CREEPY PROFESSOR
              Pfft good luck with that man.

                         KEVIN
              I'm sorry?

                         CREEPY PROFESSOR
              I've been trying to get that all
              semester, you know show her how
              good old school can really be, am I
              right bro?

Creepy professor puts his hand up for a high-five.

kevin just looks at him and shakes his head.

                         KEVIN
              No, just no.

Kevin just walks away.

                         CREEPY PROFESSOR
              Alright I'll catch you later man.

16   EXT. UNIVERSITY PARKING LOT DAY

        Kevin walks up to his car and puts his bag in the backseat
        then pulls out his phone.

                                                    (CONTINUED)

                         KEVIN
          5 new voice mails really?

Todd comes up to the car.

                         TODD
          Hey man, what's up?

                         KEVIN
          Not too much, dude look at this
          shit five voice mails and 10 texts.

                         TODD
          From who, you got a new girly I
          don't know about?

                         KEVIN
          No they're all from Simon although
          I did just hit on that hot
          Assistant in the library.

                         TODD
          That's my boy, get her number.

Kevin pulls out the piece of paper.

                         KEVIN
          Yeah, I sure did buddy, her name is
          Kristen.

                         TODD
          Sweet, so who's Simon?

                         KEVIN
          The kid from the project I'm doing.

                         TODD
          Oh the addict?

                         KEVIN
          Yeah I've been ignoring him all day
          because I fought with my mom about
          it the other night.

                         TODD
          Well what are the voice mails.

                         KEVIN
          I'm not sure let's find out.

Kevin puts his phone on speaker and dials voicemail

                              PHONE
                    Please enter your password then
                    press pound.

          Kevin types in the password

                              PHONE
                    You have five new voice messages,
                    first voice message.

                              SIMON
                    Hey dude, I need a ride call me
                    back it's Simon.

                              PHONE
                    Next message

                              SIMON
                    Dude come on call me back, really
                    need a ride.

                              PHONE
                    Next message.

                              SIMON
                    Man what the fuck answer your phone
                    I'm not trying to borrow your
                    money.

                              PHONE
                    Next message.

                              SIMON
                    WHAT THE FUCK, I know you're
                    sitting around with your cool queer
                    friends laughing at me calling,
                    real nice, fuck you asshole.

                              PHONE
                    Next message.

                              SIMON
                    Dude you think you're fucking
                    better than me, using me for your
                    project then when I call just
                    ignore me, wow man real cool kid
                    you are, you're a piece of shit.

                              PHONE
                    End of new messages.

          Kevin hangs up the phone and moves to the text messages.

                                              (CONTINUED)

                         TODD
          Wow, is that how he talks to you.

                         KEVIN
          Not usually, only when he hasn't
          gotten high lately.

                         TODD
          Look man, I know you're trying to
          help but maybe you should think
          about this.

                         KEVIN
          These texts are ridiculous, just
          him telling me to call him and that
          I'm the asshole.

Kevin's phone goes off.

                         TODD
          Is that him?

                         KEVIN
          Yeah, let's see how this is going
          to go.

Kevin picks up the phone on speaker.

                         KEVIN
          Hello.

                         SIMON
          Dude what the fuck, can't answer
          your phone?

                         KEVIN
          No, not when I'm in class.

                         SIMON
          Yeah, I'm sure you were in class
          ALL day.

                         KEVIN
          Anyway, what's this big emergency.

                         SIMON
          I just need to a ride to go make
          some money and it's kind of time
          sensitive so that's why I was
          getting pissed.

                    KEVIN
          I thought you got paid today.

                    SIMON
          Yeah, and?

                    KEVIN
          So if you have money why do you
          need a ride to get more?

                    SIMON
          Because my buddy fronted me a
          few pills so I have to pay him for
          that and another one.

                    KEVIN
          So you owe this guy 240?

                    SIMON
          No I owe him 280, and I was hoping
          to get two this time around to last
          me. Dude it's the last time I'll
          ask you for money.

                    KEVIN
          Wait a minute, you said you weren't
          going to ask me for money.

                    SIMON
          I might not need to but I might
          come up a little short.

                    KEVIN
          Pfft how the fuck is that my
          problem.

                    SIMON
          It's not I guess if you want to be
          a dick.

                    KEVIN
          You're not making much of a case
          for me to help you, and where am I
          giving you a ride.

                    SIMON
          Just meet me at my house I'll
          explain it when you get here.

                    KEVIN
          Yeah, alright but I'm not loaning
          you money.

                         SIMON
                Whatever just hurry up.

                         KEVIN
                I'll get there when I get there.

Kevin hangs up the phone angrily.

                         TODD
                Dude you're not really going over
                there are you.

                         KEVIN
                I shouldn't but I technically do
                need footage and maybe I can
                convince him to stop doing this.

                         TODD
                Man, I don't know.

                         KEVIN
                What?

                         TODD
                Nothing man just be careful I'm
                worried about ya bro.

                         KEVIN
                Thanks, but I need to do this.

                         TODD
                I'll see you tomorrow man, then you
                have to tell me about Kristen.

Kevin goes from looking stressed to cracking a smile.

                         KEVIN
                Deal.

Todd walks away.

Kevin gets in his car and starts it but doesn't drive away.

Kevin takes out the piece of paper and his phone and texts
Kristen

                         KEVIN
                      (Voice Over)
                Hey.

                         KRISTEN
                      (Voice Over)
                Hey.

                        KEVIN
                     (Voice Over)
               Missed you already, plus wanted to
               make sure you gave me a real
               number.

                        KRISTEN
                     (Voice Over)
               Aw, of course it's a real number,
               I'm glad you decided to text me.

                        KEVIN
                     (Voice Over)
               Needed a smile, kind of stressed.

                        KRISTEN
                     (Voice Over)
               Well any time you're wanting me to
               suck your cock I'm here.

Kevin looks at the phone in surprise.

                        KEVIN
                     (Voice Over)
               Don't you want dinner first, ha ha
               ha.

                        KRISTEN
                     (Voice Over)
               Oh my god, I mean when your stuck
               and want to talk. Embarrassed
               Emoji.

Kevin smiles

                        KEVIN
                     (Voice Over)
               Auto correct strikes again, well
               you definitely made me smile so
               thank you for that.

                        KRISTEN
                     (Voice Over)
               Anytime,I'm glad I could help,
               Smiley face Emoji.

                        KEVIN
                     (Voice Over)
               Me too, I'll text you later I have
               to get more footage.

                              KRISTEN
                           (Voice Over)
                    Alright, I can't wait.

Kevin still smiling puts the phone in the cup holder and
backs the car up.

EXT SIMON'S PORCH DAY

Kevin Drives up and parks in the front yard

Simon is sitting on the porch with a box smoking a
cigarette.

                              SIMON
                    Hey there he is, what's up
                    Hollywood.

Kevin get's out of the car and walks up to the porch.

                              KEVIN
                    Really?

                              SIMON
                    Really what?

                              KEVIN
                    An hour ago my phone was full of
                    angry messages and now you want to
                    be all buddy buddy.

                              SIMON
                    Oh, that? I was just stressing man,
                    don't take it so personally.

                              KEVIN
                    What's with the box.

                              SIMON
                    This is all the stuff we're going
                    to sell at the pawn shop.

                              KEVIN
                    Wow, this is a lot of DVDs

                              SIMON
                    Yeah, and my guitar.

                              KEVIN
                    I thought you loved playing?

                    SIMON
          I still have my acoustic.

                    JORDAN
          Until you sell that next week.

                    SIMON
          If I have to then oh well, at least
          I'm not taking your money.

                    JORDAN
          Are you high? I gave you half of my
          paycheck today.

                    SIMON
          Dude shut up and I told you, you're
          going to get it back so quit
          bitching.

                    JORDAN
               (sarcastically)
          Yeah, okay.

                    SIMON
          I told you man, I got a fool proof
          plan that will earn what I owe you
          plus interest.

                    KEVIN
          What's this plan?

                    SIMON
          Help me put this crap in your car
          and I'll tell ya on the way, we
          have to get there before they
          close.

                    KEVIN
          Where is this place?

                    SIMON
          About a ten minute drive over in
          Tinder.

                    KEVIN
          Alright, let's do this, got
          everything?

                    SIMON
          Yup, you want a butt?

                    KEVIN
          You ask me that every time I see
          you, and the answer is still no.

                    SIMON
          You'll come around.

Kevin and Simon get in the car.

Kevin starts the car and rolls down his windows.

                    KEVIN
          Are you coming with us Jordan?

                    JORDAN
          As much fun as it sounds like I
          think not.

                    SIMON
          you're missing out man.

                    JORDAN
          Yeah, well you'll have to have fun
          for me.

                    SIMON
          Oh I always have fun.

Kevin and Simon drive away.

INT LIGHTNING PAWN DAY

Kevin and Simon drag the box up to the counter and set it
down.

                    JOHNNY PAWN
          Hey there guys welcome to Lightning
          Pawn, how can I help you today.

Kevin looks around the store

                    SIMON
          Hey, I was hoping to unload this
          box of movies today, there's over
          300 and also an original Nintendo.

                    JOHNNY PAWN
          Alright alright, let see if we can
          make a deal, I'll give you 200 for
          the box.

                              SIMON
                    200? Come on for an original
                    Nintendo and all these movies.

                              KEVIN
                    A Nintendo? Wheres your Guitar

                              SIMON
                    I left it in the car, not quite
                    desperate enough to get rid of it.

                              KEVIN
                    Where did you get the Nintendo?

                              SIMON
                    It's my brother's ex girlfriend's

                              JOHNNY PAWN
                    Everyone has Xbox ones now.

                              SIMON
                    Come on, it's a collectors piece,
                    can't you go up to 250.

                              JOHNNY PAWN
                    I don't know it's hard to sell that
                    kind of stuff.

          Kevin is looking in the cameras.

                              JOHNNY PAWN
                    See anything you like there?

                              KEVIN
                    I'm just curious why you sell
                    stolen property.

                              JOHNNY PAWN
                    Whoa now that's ridiculous.

                              KEVIN
                    Well there's the sign outside your
                    door.

                              JOHNNY PAWN
                    It's a joke, I run an honest
                    business here.

                              KEVIN
                    Then why is it you have a camera
                    that's got some of the numbers
                    filed off and says right on the
                    side property of GFHS.

                                                    (CONTINUED)

                              JOHNNY PAWN
                    It was a donation.

Johnny starts to get fidgety

                              KEVIN
                    I highly doubt that and I remember
                    reading the media lab at the high
                    school was robbed, odd coincidence.

                              JOHNNY PAWN
                    Alright, here.

Johnny opens the register and hands Simon a stack of money.

                              JOHNNY PAWN
                    There, 400 now get him out of my
                    store. He's bad for business.

                              KEVIN
                    Glad we could get a good deal and
                    in lightning fast time no less.

                              JOHNNY PAWN
                    Well that's our name.
                    Have a great day.

Simon and Kevin walk out the door

Guys in ski masks walk past them with T.V.s

Simon and Kevin get in the car.

EXT LIGHTNING PAWN DAY

Kevin and Simon pull up to the pawn shop and park the car.

                              SIMON
                    This is the place.

                              KEVIN
                    Really?

Kevin looks around and steps out of the car.

Simon unloads the box and the guitar.

                              SIMON
                    Hey want to give me a hand with
                    this box.

                              KEVIN
                    Oh yeah, sure.

Kevin walks over and picks up one end of the box.

                              KEVIN
                    Holy cow.

                              SIMON
                    Yeah, there's a lot of dvds

                              KEVIN
                    I don't know this place seems a
                    little sketchy don't you think.

                              SIMON
                    What makes you think that?

                              KEVIN
                    Well the motto for one.

Kevin points to the sign on the window.

                              KEVIN
                    "We pay top dollar for your stolen
                    goods."

                              SIMON
                    I'm sure it's a joke, now let's get
                    this box inside it's getting heavy.

They bring the box inside the door.

20   INT KEVIN'S CAR DAY

Simon and Kevin are driving along

Simon is counting the money and making a phone call

                              SIMON
                    Hey Bud, what's good?

                              SIMON
                    Yeah, I have the money, where can I
                    meet you?

                              SIMON
                    Same place, alright sounds good see
                    you in 45 minutes.

Simon hangs up his phone.

Kevin keeps looking at his.

                         KEVIN
          Hey man, are we all good?

                         SIMON
          Am I keeping you from a hot date or
          something.

                         KEVIN
          Actually yeah you are.

                         SIMON
                    (Annoyed)
          Wow guy, well don't let me keep you
          any longer director sir. I'm
          meeting him here so good luck with
          your big date.

Simon gets out of the car.

Kevin starts the car and rolls down the window.

                         KEVIN
          Wait, you mean here in public?

                         SIMON
          Yeah, why do you give a shit, don't
          you have somewhere to be.

                         KEVIN
          Yeah, I might be busy the next
          couple weeks with midterm studying.

                         SIMON
          Yeah whatever man, see ya whenever.

Kevin goes to speak but decides he's late enough and rolls
up the window and drives off.

Kevin calls Kristen.

                         KRISTEN
          Hey.

                         KEVIN
          Hey, sorry I'm still coming just
          ran a few minutes behind.

                         KRISTEN
          It's alright, where are you?

                         KEVIN
          Down the road I'll be there in like
          5 minutes.

                              KRISTEN
                    Alright, you want me to get us a
                    table?

                              KEVIN
                    Great Idea, I'll be there as fast
                    as I can.

                              KRISTEN
                    Just drive safe.

                              KEVIN
                    I will, see you soon.

Kevin drops the phone and hits the gas.

21   INT KEVIN'S LIVING ROOM LATE AT NIGHT

Kevin walks in the door and takes his shoes off.

Kevin looks over and sees his mom asleep on the chair.

Kevin looks at her and smiles and covers her up with a
blanket and turns out the light.

22   INT. RESTAURANT NIGHT

Kevin comes in the front door kind of out of breath.

                              HOSTESS
                    Hi, welcome to first impressions,
                    just one?

Kevin catches his breathe and stands up.

                              KEVIN
                    No, I'm meeting a girl.

                              HOSTESS
                    Alright, do you know where she's
                    sitting.

Kevin scans the restaurant a couple times.

Kristen stands up and waves him over.

                              KEVIN
                    Ah, she's right there.

                              HOSTESS
                    You can head right over there, here
                    you go.

Hostess hands Kevin a menu.

Kevin walks over to the Table.

                    KEVIN
          Wow.

                    KRISTEN
          Wow good, or wow bad?

Kevin smiles.

                    KEVIN
          Definitely wow good, you look
          absolutely amazing.

Kristen blushes

Waitress walks over.

                    WAITRSSS
          Hey guys can i get you something to
          drink, our specials tonight are the
          Cosby, the resting bitch face and
          the yes dear those jeans do make
          you fat shot.

                    KEVIN
          Hmm what do you have on draft?

                    WAITRSSS
          For draft we have the Sam's
          seasonal which just switched to
          October-fest, we have Boston Lager
          and we have a new brew called
          Abductee, It's a encounter of the
          3rd kind for your taste buds.

                    KEVIN
          That sounds really good I'll go
          with that

                    WAITRESS
          And for you miss?

                    KRISTEN
          I'll have the same.

                    WAITRESS
          Alright great I'll be right back
          with those.

The waitress walks away leaving just Kristen and Kevin
sitting in a awkward silence.

                              KEVIN
                    So tell me about yourself.

                              KRISTEN
                    What do you want to know?

          Kevin makes eye contact with her and smiles.

                              KEVIN
                    Everything. How old are you, where
                    are you from.

                              KRISTEN
                    Well I'm 22, I grew up in Seattle.

                              KEVIN
                    Seattle? Wow, go Seahawks.

          Kevin fidgets nervously

                              KRISTEN
                    Um, yeah I don't really watch
                    football.

                              KEVIN
                    Ah.

          they sit there awkwardly silent.

                              KEVIN
                          (T.V. promo voice)
                    Who killed Rosie Larsen?

                              KRISTEN
                    Wait, what did you say?

          Kevin looks up at her.

                              KEVIN
                    Oh, sorry when I'm nervous I have a
                    tendency to quote T.V. or Movies,
                    that was from..

          Kristen cuts him off.

                              KRISTEN
                    The Killing, on AMC.

                              KEVIN
                    You know it?

                              KRISTEN
                Know it, it's one of my favorites.

                              KEVIN
                No Way, Mine too.

                              KRISTEN
                I can't get enough of it, I mean it
                just kept you guessing. AMC really
                gets great shows.

                              KEVIN
                I know right, I mean for me it
                doesn't get better then Bryan
                Cranston and Vince Gilligan.

                              KRISTEN
                Right, Oh my god, Vince is one of
                my favorite writers, the way He
                weaves it all together and the
                characters are just so easy to
                relate to for me.

                              KEVIN
                Oh my gosh, so you've wanted to
                cook meth too? I thought it was
                just me.

They both burst out laughing.

Their beers come and they keep talking and laughing

A few beers later Kevin's phone goes off.

                              KEVIN
                Oh, sorry let me just check that.

Kevin reads a text from his mom.

                              KEVIN
                It's my mom.

                              KRISTEN
                Good news?

                              KEVIN
                She's just checking up on me,
                things have been a little crazy
                lately and I forgot to tell her I'd
                be out this late.

                                              (CONTINUED)

                              KRISTEN
                    Aw, you're mom sounds sweet.

                              KEVIN
                    She is.

                              KRISTEN
                    What about your dad?

                              KEVIN
                    He split a long time ago, it's just
                    been me and her, I think she's
                    afraid I'll leave her too.

                              KRISTEN
                    I'm sorry, I know what you're going
                    through, It's just been me and my
                    dad.

                              KEVIN
                    What happened?

                              KRISTEN
                    She died when I was young.

                              KEVIN
                    Shit, I'm sorry. That has to be
                    tough.

                              KRISTEN
                    My dad took it really hard, He
                    hasn't been himself and now I worry
                    about him since he is 5 states
                    away.

                              KEVIN
                    I felt that burden too, after high
                    school I wanted to stay and help my
                    mom and I'll never forget what she
                    said.

                              KRISTEN
                    What did she say?

                              KEVIN
                    She said the best way to help her
                    is to chase my dreams and be the
                    best person I can be.

                              KRISTEN
                    Aww, your mother sounds sweet.

                         KEVIN
              Yeah, she is, she's worried that
              this project is having a negative
              effect on me.

                         KRISTEN
              Is it?

                         KEVIN
              I'm not sure, It's raised
              insecurities and can get dangerous.
              I just feel like I can get through
              to Simon.

                         KRISTEN
              Why is it so important to you that
              you would put your life in danger
              for a stranger?

                         KEVIN
              I was young when my father left, I
              couldn't help him but if I help
              Simon it can make up for that.

                         KRISTEN
              Some people can't be saved, they
              don't want to be saved.

                         KEVIN
              Maybe, but everyone deserves a shot
              at redemption, no is ever too far
              gone.

Kristen grabs Kevin's hand across the table.

Kevin looks up into her eyes.

                         KRISTEN
              Just be careful, don't get pulled
              down with him.

Kevin meets her gaze for a minute and then nods.

EXT UNIVERSITY PARK MORNING

Kevin walks up to John with the usual hot coffee

Kevin takes a deep breathe and exhales.

                         KEVIN
              I can see my breath today,

John is looking at a picture and quickly tucks it away and
takes his coffee.

(CONTINUED)

                         KEVIN
               Morning John, What are you looking
               at?

                         JOHN
               Oh, nothing, it was uh, just a
               picture I've kept from a long time
               ago.

                         KEVIN
               I love crisp mornings like this,
               Frost on the ground, fresh air.

                         JOHN
               Well someone had a good night sleep
               last night.

                         KEVIN
               Yeah you could say that.

Kristen walks by and smiles at Kevin.

Kevin waves her over and smiles.

                         JOHN
               Ahh I see.

Kristen walks over to John and Kevin.

Kevin Hugs her.

                         KEVIN
               Hey Beautiful.

Kristen shivers in the morning cold.

                         KRISTEN
               Good morning.

Kevin turns to John.

                         KEVIN
               John, this is Kristen.

                         JOHN
               Hello Kristen it is nice to meet
               you.

Kristen shakes John's hand.

Kristen and Kevin Sit on the bench.

(CONTINUED

                              KRISTEN
            So how did everything go with your
            mother?

                              KEVIN
            Oh, we haven't really talked about
            too much, but we're talking.

                              JOHN
            Things going better with her?

                              KEVIN
            Getting there, she worries when I'm
            out late, She just assumes I'm
            hanging out with Simon.

                              JOHN
            I haven't heard you talk about him
            in a while.

                              KEVIN
            Well I haven't seen him in a few
            weeks, and since then no texts or
            calls.

                              JOHN
            Is that a good thing?

                              KEVIN
            Honestly I have a lot less stress,
            He is just so impulsive even sober,
            He doesn't think about what he
            says. I remember one night I
            thought we were going to get shot.

                              KRISTEN
            Oh my god, really?

                              KEVIN
            It was weird, He had ripped off
            this Junkie and got into a verbal
            spat with him, next thing I know
            there is a car driving around the
            neighborhood that night without
            headlights.

                              JOHN
            So did you call the cops?

                              KEVIN
            No, Genius went there with a stick
            shouting into the dark.

                              KRISTEN
                    That's crazy.

                              KEVIN
                    Yeah you're telling me, my heart
                    was racing, he wasn't thinking
                    about how a drive-by could endanger
                    everyone in the house.

Kevin smiles at Kristen

                              KEVIN
                    So I made a decision to surround
                    myself with better company.

Kevin hugs Kristen and they both smile.

John pulls out a picture of a young woman.

                              JOHN
                    You two remind me so much of me and
                    my wife.

                              KEVIN
                    Oh yeah? Say how come you never
                    talk about her?

                              JOHN
                    It's a boring tale.

                              KRISTEN
                    Aw, come on we would love to hear
                    it.

                              JOHN
                    Really?

                              KEVIN
                    Yeah man, I'm curious.

Kevin and Kristen Sit close to each other.

                              JOHN
                    Well, I'm not sure where to start
                    from.

                              KEVIN
                    What's the moment you knew you were
                    in love with her.

John stares into the eyes of the woman in the photo.

John smiles and chuckles.

                                                    (CONTINUED)

                              JOHN
                    Well that's an easy one.

INT GYMNASIUM NIGHT

The gym is full of young adults dressed in military
uniforms.

                              JOHN
                          (Voice Over)
                    I had just finished basic, we had
                    started dating 6 months before, I
                    hadn't seen her in over two months.

A young John congratulates other Marines and then see's
Helen walking though the crowd.

John smiles.

John walks up to her.

                         YOUNGER JOHN
                    Excuse me miss

                              HELEN
                    Yes?

                         YOUNGER JOHN
                    I can't help but notice you're
                    sitting alone.

                              HELEN
                    I'm waiting for someone

                         YOUNGER JOHN
                    Well I'm here now so lets make your
                    dreams come true.

                              HELEN
                    I'm waiting for my boyfriend.

                         YOUNGER JOHN
                    What's this boyfriend like.

                              HELEN
                    Well he's about six feet, brown
                    hair, he's kind of a nerd.

                         YOUNGER JOHN
                    Sounds boring, you should dump him.

                                              (CONTINUED)

                         HELEN
          Can't

                      YOUNGER JOHN
          What's keeping you there.

                         HELEN
          The sex, its unbelievable.

                      YOUNGER JOHN
          Really?

John gets closer to her.

                         HELEN
          Well I mean kind of but He's quick
          on the trigger, only last a minute
          or two.

Helen turns and looks at John with a big wide smile

John's trying to keep a straight face but they both start
laughing.

John hugs Helen tight.

                      YOUNGER JOHN
          I missed you so much, you look as
          beautiful as the day I first saw
          you.

                         HELEN
          Ah yes you were smooth that night,
          stumbling up to me in the bar to
          say what.

                      YOUNGER JOHN
          Hey babe, wanna dance?

                         HELEN
          My Poet

                      YOUNGER JOHN
          What can I say, I'm just full of
          charm.

Helen smiles.

                         HELEN
          You're full of something alright.

They both chuckle

John just stares into Helen's eyes smiling.

                                        (CONTINUED

                         HELEN
              What?

John smiles wide and keeps looking at her eyes.

                         HELEN
              What is it?

                         YOUNGER JOHN
              Those eyes, it's been way too long
              since I've seen those eyes.

Helen smiles big.

                         YOUNGER JOHN
              I missed you so much

                         HELEN
              I missed you too, I'm so proud of
              you.

                         YOUNGER JOHN
              So, how do you like the new look?

John flexes a muscle.

                         HELEN
              Wow my strong man has some muscles
              now.

                         YOUNGER JOHN
              That's right babe now how about
              that drink.

                         HELEN
              I don't think I can do that.

                         YOUNGER JOHN
              Oh come on why not?

Helen puts John's hand on her stomach

                         HELEN
              because I don't think the baby
              would like it.

John looks at his hand on her stomach and then at her
shocked.

                         YOUNGER JOHN
              Are you saying You're...

Helen smiles nodding.

                                        (CONTINUED)

                              YOUNGER JOHN
                         Who's the father?

Helen slaps him laughing

John grabs her tight and kisses her.

John stands up with a bottle.

                              YOUNGER JOHN
                         Hey everyone, Guess what I'm going
                         to be a father.

The crowd cheers and his friends all come to congratulate
him.

Back to present day

John wipes a tear from his eye.

                              JOHN
                         That was the happiest day of my
                         life.

Kevin and Kristen put a hand on John's shoulder.

John sobs lightly.

                              KRISTEN
                         It will be alright.

                              JOHN
                         I'm sorry, I just really miss my
                         son.

                              KEVIN
                         I'm sure he misses you too.

                              KRISTEN
                         What would you say to him right
                         now. Just picture him and talk.

John looks up toward Kevin.

                              JOHN
                         I would look in the eye and tell
                         him how proud I am of the man he
                         has become.

                              KEVIN
                         I'm sure he knows John.

Kevin's phone rings

                         KEVIN
          Oh great, this should be good.

                         KRISTEN
          Who is it?

Kevin answers the phone and puts it on speaker.

                         SIMON
          Dude you got to help me out.

                         KEVIN
          I don't got to do jack shit
          asshole.

                         SIMON
          what's with the fucking attitude
          kid.

                         KEVIN
          Did you just call me kid?

                         SIMON
          My bad, but you're acting like a
          little bitch, want me to lift up
          your skirt and tickle your pussy
          for ya?

                         KEVIN
          Wow, you really do have a fucked up
          version of asking for help.

                         SIMON
          Fuck off man just give me some
          money I've got a huge problem.

                         KEVIN
          Well there ya go the first steps
          admitting it.

                         SIMON
          Not that, I was supposed to sell
          some for Carlos and I would get a
          free one.

                         KEVIN
          Yes, I remember your stupid plan,
          what about it?

                         SIMON
          I had a wicked bad night and just
          did too many now I owe him like a
          thousand dollars or the product
          back.

                                        (CONTINUED)

                         KEVIN
            Aww, what a sad story, it's your
            own fault pal, and I'm not giving
            you a grand. You almost got me
            thrown in jail.

                         SIMON
            Yeah I get it, I'm just a project
            to you, a dumb fucking junkie
            whatever, I thought you wanted to
            save me.

                         KEVIN
            I did, I tried to help you at my
            own personal risk and financial
            hardship but guess what you didn't
            want my help.

                         SIMON
            Dude I can change after this come
            on.

                         KEVIN
            Nah man, you won't you're just
            going to keep taking from people
            and taking and not giving a shit
            what happens to anyone including
            your own younger brother, did you
            think about him when cooked up this
            plan to sell shit?

                         SIMON
            Ah you know what, screw you keep
            your money and just forget about
            us, don't pretend you give a shit,
            thanks for using us for your
            project.

                         KEVIN
            Hey ass, I did care and don't throw
            your brothers future away just
            because you don't have one, good
            luck finding a thousand bucks I
            truly hope he breaks your fucking
            legs.

Kevin throws the phone and smashes it on the ground.

Kristen puts her hand on Kevin's shoulder.

                         KRISTEN
            Are you okay?

                                            (CONTINUED

                          KEVIN
              He's so Frustrating.

Kevin shakes his head.

                          KEVIN
                       (Voice Over)
              Was He right though?

Kevin sits down on the bench and just thinks in silence.

                          KRISTEN
              Hey, come back to us.

                          KEVIN
              I just thought.

                          KRISTEN
              You just thought what?

Kevin stands up frustrated and paces.

                          KEVIN
              I wanted to help, to make a
              difference.

                          JOHN
              You have made a huge difference.

                          KEVIN
              How do you figure, He's still a
              Junkie and I almost got arrested.

                          JOHN
              You've helped me Kevin, you've
              given me friendship when everyone
              else walked by.

                          KRISTEN
              See, maybe you didn't help the
              person you thought but you helped
              someone.

Kevin still looks disappointed

                          JOHN
              What else has this quest really
              been about for you?

                          KEVIN
              My father.

Kevin shakes his head and looks toward the broken phone on
the ground.

                    KEVIN
          I thought If I could understand
          and help Simon that maybe I could
          help my father.

Kevin looks away from John and Kristen and wipes a tear from
his eye.

Kristen walks over and hugs Kevin.

                    KEVIN
          We should get going, we have to go
          pick up my camera and my mom before
          the presentation.

                    JOHN
          Good luck today.

                    KEVIN
          Thanks John, and you've helped me
          out too. You've been like the
          father I was missing.

John chokes up.

                    JOHN
          We should talk after your
          presentation.

                    KEVIN
          Alright. you're welcome to come
          watch you know.

                    JOHN
          I wouldn't miss it for the world...
          son.

Kevin smirks and him and Kristen walk away.

25   INT. SIMON'S HOUSE MORNING

Simon looks at his phone and throws it on the chair.

Jordan is walking in and out of his room packing things.

Simon walks over to the table to prepare a pill.

                    SIMON
          Can you believe that piece of shit?
          After all we did for him and his
          project.

Simon cuts the pill and crushes it.

                              SIMON
                    He used us and now when I need a
                    favor he's nowhere to be found, You
                    can't trust anyone in this world
                    Jordan.

Simon blows his nose to clear his nostril

                              SIMON
                    Everyone's got their own fucking
                    agenda so let that be a lesson to
                    you.

Jordan zips up his duffel bag and puts it by the front door.

                              JORDAN
                    That's the pot calling the kettle
                    black to the extreme.

Simon jams one pill and then immediately gets another one
ready.

                              SIMON
                    What's that supposed to mean.

                              JORDAN
                    Everyone's got their own agenda to
                    screw you over? that's what you do,
                    you've made a career out of
                    dragging other people into your
                    shit.

Jordan lights up a joint and takes a drag.

                              JORDAN
                    You always have someone else to
                    blame, don't you think it's
                    convenient you're never taking
                    responsibility for your own fuck
                    ups.

Simon jams another big line.

                              SIMON
                    What do you know about taking
                    responsibility, where's your life
                    going that's so great.

                              JORDAN
                    I don't know, college somewhere
                    away from here.

Jordan takes another drag and holds it for a second before
releasing.

(CONTINUED)

                              JORDAN
                    But you know what I take
                    responsibility for every time I
                    fall. I don't blame you, I don't
                    blame mom, I don't bury my head in
                    a pill and cry about how the world
                    is out to get me.

Simon tips his head back and laughs.

                              SIMON
                    You talk a lot of righteous
                    bullshit for someone smoking a
                    joint right now.

Jordan looks at the joint and shrugs as he exhales.

Simon takes a notepad out and continues writing something on
the page.

                              JORDAN
                    Well yeah, I mean I'm a writer it
                    helps my process.

Simon looks up at Jordan and cracks a smile.

Simon and Jordan both start laughing.

                              JORDAN
                    I will give you credit though, you
                    were right about something.

                              SIMON
                    What's that?

                              JORDAN
                    This world we live in now, with so
                    much negativity eating the airwaves
                    we all have our vices and pot is
                    mine.

                              SIMON
                    So, you're not going to help me are
                    you?

Jordan leans forward taking one last hit and holding it.

                              JORDAN
                    No, this time it has to be you to
                    clean this up brother, take some
                    responsibility and make this right.

Simon looks down letting the words sink in.

Jordan cracks a small laugh

                    JORDAN
          Kind of a mind fuck isn't it.

                    SIMON
          What's that?

                    JORDAN
          Well you should be telling me all
          this, I'm the younger brother.

Simon chuckles softly.

Jordan finishes his joint and stands up

Simon stands up.

                    SIMON
          Where are you going?

                    JORDAN
          Stuff's getting a little too heated
          for me so I'm going to Kevin's
          presentation then probably going to
          stay my friends until this blows
          over.

                    SIMON
          He was right, I have been a shitty
          brother. I shouldn't have gotten
          you involved in this and I am
          sorry.

                    JORDAN
          You're not a shitty brother, you
          just got lost. Family's supposed to
          be a pain in the ass.

                    SIMON
          I love you bud, I mean that. When
          everyone else gave up on me you
          still stuck with me.

Simon hugs Jordan.

                    JORDAN
          I love you too man, good luck.

Simon hands Jordan a envelope.

                        SIMON
            If I text you today, will you give
            this to Kevin.

Jordan nods.

Jordan grabs a bag and walks out the door.

Simon sits in the chair and looks at the pills lying out.

26   INT COLLEGE CLASSROOM DAY

Kids are talking in their seats and filing in.

Kevin is stand in the back talking to Kristen and his
mother.

                        KRISTEN
                Are you nervous?

                        KEVIN
                Well just a little.

                        KRISTEN
                You're going to do great.

                        MRS. BROOKE
                Yeah, you're going to crush it
                honey.

                        KEVIN
                There's a lot of people here.

The professor walks to the podium

                        PROFESSOR STARNE
                Alright settle down guys. Today's
                presenter is Kevin Brooke.

The class claps.

                        KEVIN
                Well here we go, wish me luck.

                        MRS. BROOKE
                Good luck

Kevin hugs his mom and Kristen and starts to walk to the
front of the class.

Jordan shows up and stands in the back not far from Kristen
and Kevin's mom.

Kevin stands at the podium getting his video ready.

Jordan walks up to Mrs. Brooke

                    JORDAN
          Hello mam.

Mrs. Brooke turns to see Jordan.

                    MRS. BROOKE
          Oh hello, are we in the way?

                    JORDAN
          No mam I know your son and wanted
          to introduce myself.

Kevin looks up and sees Jordan shaking his mothers hand.

                    JORDAN
          My name is Jordan Baker, Simon is
          my brother.

Mrs. Brooke doesn't know what to say.

                    JORDAN
          I know your son was paying Simon
          and that caused some tension, but
          He was doing it for me, trying to
          help so I just wanted to say thank
          you.

Jordan starts to walk away.

                    MRS. BROOKE
          Wait, stay and watch with us.

                    JORDAN
          Really?

                    MRS. BROOKE
          Yes, please sit.

Kevin sees this while setting up the laptop.

Jordan nods his head towards Kevin.

Kevin waves with a smile.

Kevin takes one last look around the room as if he's looking
for someone.

                    PROFESSOR STARNE
          Are you ready to start Kevin?

                                        (CONTINUED)

                         KEVIN
               Yes professor I think I am.

Kevin looks up at the class.

                         KEVIN
               Hello everyone, my name is Kevin
               and I did a documentary as my
               project. I had planned to a report
               on the hospital which is facing
               multiple claims of negligence.
               While in the waiting room of the ER
               I saw a young man in very poor
               condition being ignored by doctors
               even pushed to the side simply
               because he was a drug addict.

Kevin puts up a screenshot of Simon

                         KEVIN
               This is Simon Baker. Before I start
               I just want to say that sometimes
               you meet people, people that change
               you. Some for the worse and some
               for the better.

Kevin looks around the Room to Simon's brother Jordan and
Kristen.

Behind Kristen John enters the room.

Everyone turns to see him and whispers start.

                         PROFESSOR STARNE
               Quiet down class. Continue with
               your project Kevin.

Kevin switches to a video clip.

                         KEVIN
               This clip I'm about to show you is
               Simon getting high.

Kevin rolls a clip of Simon happily snorting a pill
and leaning back becoming very relaxed.

Kevin pauses just as Simon is making a funny face.

The class laughs.

                         PROFESSOR STARNE
               Quiet class.

                         KEVIN
          He could be funny, Simon is
          actually extremely intelligent and
          I was almost fooled by it. Addicts
          will manipulate whoever they have
          to get a fix and will just as
          easily toss that person aside after
          they get what they want.

Behind Kevin Simon's goofy face vanishes and a dashboard is
replaced.

                         KEVIN
          My research almost landed me in
          Jail.

Kevin looks up to his mother who is shocked.

                         KEVIN
          This next clip will show you.

Kevin hits play and sits down.

INT KEVIN'S CAR NIGHT.

The car is dark, the camera pans up and we can see a
streetlight in the distance. Kevin is wearing a Go pro

Kevin lets out a breath that fogs up the windshield

Kevin pans to the backseat where Jordan is writing in a
notebook.

                         KEVIN
          Does he always take this long?

                         JORDAN
          Yup I'm afraid so, but at least he
          left the car. One night He left me
          on some random ass road for about
          an hour.

                         KEVIN
          That had to suck.

                         JORDAN
          Meh, gave me great Ideas for a
          horror story.

                         KEVIN
                    (nervously)
          Ha, always the optimist.

A branch snaps outside.

Kevin wheels around looking everywhere.

Jordan can't help but crack up.

Kevin takes some deep breathes and starts to laugh.

>   JORDAN
>   Jumpy are we?

>   KEVIN
>   Ass, this is how B horror movies
>   start.

They both laugh.

Suddenly Simon opens the door scaring both of them.

>   SIMON
>   What's up bitches.

>   KEVIN
>   You scared the shit out of me man,
>   what the fuck took so long? what
>   happened to in and out.

>   SIMON
>   Meh, he offered me some blow and I
>   didn't want to be rude.

>   KEVIN
>   (annoyed)
>   Right totally makes sense, mean
>   while we're here in the dark woods
>   about to be a victim on the show
>   Supernatural. But I'm glad you
>   weren't rude.

>   SIMON
>   Ya done?

>   KEVIN
>   Yeah, next time though I'd like all
>   the information.

>   SIMON
>   Did I leave something out?

>   KEVIN
>   Just the fact that the "little
>   drive" we had to take was actually
>   100 miles north to the Canadian
>   boarder.

Simon starts the car and the headlights come on.

(CONTINUED

Simon lights a butt.

>   SIMON
>   Come on it was a little fun.

Silence for a minute as Simon stares at Kevin.

Kevin finally looks and cracks up a little

>   KEVIN
>   Can we just get the fuck out of
>   Camp crystal lake here before Jason
>   shows up.

Everyone starts laughing

Simon drives for a few minutes down the dirt road to the
main tar and then pulls over.

>   KEVIN
>   Why are we stopping?

>   SIMON
>   I gotta count em.

>   KEVIN
>   What are you nuts, lets just do
>   that later we have a long drive
>   home.

>   SIMON
>   It'll be longer if you keep
>   interrupting me.

Simon grabs two small pill containers and pours them on to
his lap to count them.

>   KEVIN
>   That should last you some time.

>   SIMON
>   Nah these aren't mine to keep.
>   they're Carlos's to sell, I just
>   get a couple for making the pick
>   up.

Kevin still wearing the camera looks at the rear mirror and
sees headlights approaching.

>   KEVIN
>   Dude put that shit away we got
>   company.

                    SIMON
          Probably just someone driving
          through.

The headlights pull up behind them.

                    KEVIN
          Dude seriously come on.

Simon looks up.

Blue lights start to flash.

                    JORDAN
          Holy shit.

                    SIMON
          Just be cool.

Simon starts to put the pills back in the bottles.

A flashlight comes closer approaching the driver door.

Simon fumbles to get all the pills away and hands Kevin the
containers.

Kevin shoves one in the glove box

The cop is almost to the door.

Kevin freezes for a minute then shoves the one under his
ass.

Just as he pulls his hands away the flashlight beam hits the
Glovebox.

                    OFFICER
          Having some car trouble?

                    SIMON
          No sir, I dropped my butt when I
          was driving so pulled over to grab
          it.

Kevin looks up trying to control his breathing.

Simon takes a drag.

The cop looks around and at Kevin.

Kevin can hear his heart pounding

                         KEVIN
                     (voice over)
            Ah fuck we're going to jail.

                         OFFICER
            Well If you guys are sure you're
            alright then.

                         SIMON
            Yeah

The cop stands there for what seems like an eternity then
clicks the flashlight off.

                         OFFICER
            Well you kids get home safe, this
            is a bad spot to get stuck out
            here.

                         SIMON
            Yes sir, and I really appreciate
            your concern.

                         OFFICER
            You're welcome.

The cop walks back to his cruiser shuts off the blues and
drives away.

Kevin turns to Simon, then to Jordan who looks stunned.

Kevin finally exhales sharply and begins breathing heavy and
shaking.

                         SIMON
            Holy shit.

Simon hits the roof the car screaming with joy.

                         SIMON
            Woo now that was fucking rush haha.

                         KEVIN
            Really?

                         SIMON
            What, that's some great footage
            Spielberg. I can't believe you
            stashed the pills under your ass.

                         KEVIN
            Can we just go home now before our
            luck runs out.

                              SIMON
                    Good thinking.

Kevin grabs the go pro off his head and turns it off

28   INT COLLEGE CLASSROOM DAY

The class is in Aw.

                              KEVIN
                    That was the scariest moment of my
                    life and when I decided enough was
                    enough before something bad
                    happened.

Kevin sips from his water.

                              KEVIN
                    I have one more video to show you,
                    It's a little disturbing.

Kevin runs his hand through his hair.

                              KEVIN
                    There's another side to addiction
                    though, a side that is much darker
                    that people brush off as justified
                    means to choosing a life of drugs.

Kevin loads another clip up.

                              KEVIN
                    The universe has always had a
                    counterweight, Light turns to dark,
                    sunny turns to cloudy, and in this
                    case the rush of being high turns
                    into the excruciating pain of
                    withdrawal.

Kevin steps back and rolls a clip of Simon in pain from not
being able to get high.

After the clip stops Kevin looks around the room.

Jordan shakes his head in half disbelief have remembrance.

A hush falls over the classroom, slight discomfort.

On the screen is the sickly face of Simon

Kevin moves to the front to face the class.

Kevin clears his throat.

                                                    (CONTINUED

A student raises her hand shyly.

                    KEVIN
          Yes?

                    STUDENT
          Um, How long had he gone without a
          fix?

                    KEVIN
          24 hours.

The class whispers and murmurs.

                    STUDENT
          Didn't this make him want to get
          help.

                    KEVIN
          No, and there was none for him.

                    STUDENT
          I don't understand, aren't there
          clinics?

                    KEVIN
          I'll explain, there was no help for
          him because He didn't want it see
          an addict has to choose to fully
          accept that they have a problem and
          want to get better.

Kevin looks down in disappointment

                    KEVIN
          Sometimes a person is just too far
          down no matter how hard you try you
          can't help them.

Kevin looks up and catches John's eye

                    KEVIN
          And as for your other question the
          clinics are a front for more
          addiction, you get hooked on
          another painkiller to ween you off
          the other, it doesn't help anyone
          except the government. I saw people
          leave the clinic and the first
          thing they did was more pills.

Jordan looks at his phone quick and walks out.

Suddenly more and more students are getting up and rushing to the window.

Students run out to the parking lot.

29   EXT UNIVERSITY PARKING LOT DAY

Everyone runs to the parking lot watching the street.

Students are mingling and have their cell phones out videoing.

Kevin finds Kristen and his mother.

                         KEVIN
               Why is everyone so excited?

                         KRISTEN
               Look at all the police cars.

Kevin turns to look.

3 cop cars go by.

Jordan joins Kevin.

                         JORDAN
               Wow some crazy stuff going down
               somewhere.

                         KEVIN
               Yeah no shit.

A swat tank rides by and a SUV marked DEA

                         JORDAN
               They're going for Conner... and my
               brother.

                         KEVIN
               Who is Connor and how can you
               possibly know that.

                         JORDAN
               Connor is the big drug dealer aka
               Carlos, an old fart from down the
               street.

                         KEVIN
               You're kidding, could be a
               coincidence.

Jordan gets out his phone and opens it to a text.

                    KEVIN
          What's that?

Jordan passes his phone to Kevin.

                    JORDAN
          It's from Simon.

                    KEVIN
          Jordan, you were right, I'm taking
          responsibility for my mess and
          taking that old man with me,
          goodbye brother. I hope you can
          forgive me for being so shitty.
          Give the envelope to Kevin.

Kevin passes the phone back to Jordan.

                    KEVIN
          What the, that sounded like a
          suicide note or some shit, and what
          envelope.

Jordan gets out an Envelope and hands it to Kevin.

Kevin opens the envelope and unfolds the letter.

                    KEVIN
          Dear Kevin.

INT SIMON'S HOUSE EARLY MORNING

Simon sits wide awake and stares at his clipboard.

after several moments Simon moves toward the clipboard which
has a line ready to go on it.

Simon blows the pill and sits back down.

Simon paces anxiously back and forward.

Simon spots the notebook and stops for a second then keeps
pacing, deep in thought.

Simon stops again this time eyeing the pill bottle.

                    SIMON
          Fuck it.

Simon gets two pills and snorts them both.

Simon staggers backwards a little taking a deep breathe

Simons eyes water and he wipes them.

                                        (CONTINUED)

                              SIMON
                         (voice over)
                    Wow, that was a big line.

Simon walks over and counts the pills he has left.

                              SIMON
                         (voice over)
                    Shit, He's going to want pills or
                    the money which you don't have
                    either dumb ass.

Simon hesitates the does another pill.

Simon shrugs.

                              SIMON
                         (Voice over)
                    Well I'm already in the hole might
                    as well enjoy myself.

Simon starts to feel the tension melt away and loosens up

Simon sits down and picks up the notebook.

Simon flips it open and grabs a pen.

                              SIMON
                         (mockingly)
                    Write down your feelings, yes what
                    are you really thinking in your
                    brain.

                              SIMON
                         (Voice Over)
                    Alright How do I feel, hm Oh I
                    know.

Simon writes Really Fucking High!!

Simon laughs

                              SIMON
                    Well you can always get higher,
                    time for a treat.

Simon does another pill.

Simon sits back in the chair the smile melts away from his
face.

Simon can hardly move now but manages to turn his attention
back to the notebook.

Simon grabs it and a pen.

Simon writes nothing at first and then looks to the corner
of the room.

Simon sees a picture of him and brother standing with street
hockey sticks.

Simon laughs then shakes his head.

                    SIMON
          Those were some really good
          times, what happened to us.

Simon looks at the pills.

                    SIMON
          Oh, I happened.

After a moment He has a look of determination and begins to
write.

                    SIMON
               (Voice Over)
          Dear Kevin I'll start by saying
          thank you, you've been more of a
          friend to me lately than I have had
          in a long time, A friendship I took
          advantage of and didn't deserve.
          What follows next is not on you,
          Tonight sitting here flying high I
          saw a picture of me and Jordan.

Simon scribbles furiously on the paper and then looks at it.

Simon nods his head in approval and tears the page out and
sticks it in a envelope.

Simon sits back down and closes his eyes.

                    SIMON
          See I used to have a good grip on
          what I wanted, I wanted to show my
          little brother how to succeed.

Simon and Jordan are sitting there.

Simon stands up and gives Jordan a hug.

                    SIMON
          If I text you later give this to
          Kevin.

Jordan takes the envelope and nods then leaves.

Simon sits on the couch nodding to himself.

                    SIMON
                (Voice Over)
          All I can hope for now is that my
          failure can teach him to avoid
          making the same mistakes I did.
          I always told myself I was never
          out of control, it was never an
          issue but in reality I was never in
          control.

Simon pours the pills out of the container.

                    SIMON
                (Voice Over)
          Now I am taking control, I am up
          the creek and I owe a lot of money.
          Later I will call you begging for
          help for which you will say no, I
          will be an asshole because it is
          what has to happen. It's time to go
          out swinging.

Simon crushes the rest of the pills into one big line.

Simon looks at it for a second in amazement.

Simon uses a business card to straighten out the line of
powder.

Simon flips the card over and it's for a detective.

                    SIMON
          There's been a Detective Sniffing
          around lately, no pun intended.
          He's been trying to get at Carlos
          or as He is also known by the big
          Kahuna. Just like an old cop show
          the detective wants his bad guy.
          Well I'm taking down the old perv
          and the detective will get his man.

Simon clears his nostrils and breathes with anticipation.

                    SIMON
          But He won't get me, I am the
          author and I write my own ending.
          Might as well end on a high note.
          Good luck with your project.

Simon smiles wide and blows the first half a big line.

Simon's eyes water and he staggers trying to catch his breath.

Simon laughs a little and takes the last half.

Simon lays down on his bed smiling.

Simon's eyes remain wide open.

Blood slowly makes it way out of his nose.

Simons chest rises once and then falls never rising again.

The camera zooms out of a birds eye view

Sirens can be heard in the distance.

EXT. UNIVERSITY PARKING LOT DAY

Kevin is holding the letter reading.

> KEVIN
> Take care of my brother and thank
> you for friendship, your
> neighborhood friendly criminal
> Simon Baker.

Kevin stares at Jordan.

> KEVIN
> Wow, Jordan I'm sorry.

Jordan stares into space for a minute then smiles and looks at Kevin.

> JORDAN
> I'm not, because I believe he's
> finally at peace.

Jordan pats Kevin on the back.

> JORDAN
> I'm gonna go now, your presentation
> was great man.

Jordan walks away.

> KEVIN
> Thanks.

Kevin sees John who is looking toward Kristen and his mom.

Kevin walks up to John.

                              KEVIN
                    So, what did you think.

                              JOHN
                    She looks great.

John's still staring at Kevin's mom

                              KEVIN
                    I meant the presentation.

John turn's to Kevin.

                              JOHN
                    I thought it was a really powerful
                    statement. Your father would be.

                              KEVIN
                    I know.

John nods and looks back towards Kevin's mom.

                              KEVIN
                    No John, I mean I know why you
                    wanted to talk.

Kevin pulls out a ripped piece of picture and hands it to
John.

John looks down and looks at Kevin.

                              KEVIN
                    Dad.

John wells up.

John hugs Kevin.

                              JOHN
                    How long did you know?

                              KEVIN
                    Well I knew I'd seen the picture
                    you showed me before, but the real
                    giveaway was your story.

                              JOHN
                    Which story?

                              KEVIN
                    How you met her, Mom told me and
                    Kristen that same story when I
                    brought her over.

John starts to tear up.

> KEVIN
> Do you have any idea how hard it's
> been, how long I've been wondering
> and searching. My mom cries every
> night over you. She still loves
> you.

Kevin starts to get misty eyed and wipes it away chuckling.

> KEVIN
> Wow what a fucked up six months
> it's been.

> JOHN
> I wanted to tell you so many times
> before, I just I was scared.

> KEVIN
> Scared, scared of what?

> JOHN
> I fell so hard, how could I face
> you after all that.

> KEVIN
> So you thought vanishing was the
> best option.

> JOHN
> I'm sorry son.

Kevin wipes his eyes.

> KEVIN
> I missed you so much.. Dad

John hugs Kevin tight.

> JOHN
> I missed you too son, I can't tell
> you how proud of you I am.

> KEVIN
> I'm glad, that's what all this was
> about. I was hoping I could find
> you and it turns out I already had.

Todd comes walking up.

                              TODD
                    Dude that presentation was insane,
                    that go pro footage was just whoa
                    wait a second were you just hugging
                    the homeless guy?

                              KEVIN
                    I was yes.

Kevin wipes his eyes.

                              TODD
                    What's going on here bro.

                              KEVIN
                    This is my Father.

                              JOHN
                    Nice to meet you, excuse me I have
                    something I need to do.

                              TODD
                    Wow.

                              KEVIN
                    I know right, I'll catch you later.

John and Kevin walk over to Kevin's mom and Kristen.

Kristen hugs Kevin.

                              KRISTEN
                    Kev, you were great, but whats with
                    all the cops.

                              KEVIN
                    Simon, I'll explain later but I
                    want you to meet someone.

Kevin's mom turns to see John and freezes.

Kevin pats his dad on the shoulder and smiles.

                              KRISTEN
                         (whispering)
                    What's going on?

                              KEVIN
                    Just watch.

Kevin's mom tears up and cups her hand on her mouth.

(CONTINUED

                    JOHN
          Excuse me miss but I couldn't help
          noticing your standing alone.

Kevin's mom breathes sharply chuckling slightly and crying.

                    MRS. BROOKE
          Well see I'm waiting for someone, a
          husband.

John takes his wife's hands in his.

                    JOHN
          What's He like, this husband?

Mrs. brooke cracks up tears running.

                    MRS. BROOKE
          Well, He's about six feet, has a
          beard like a lions mane and He's
          kind of a nerd.

John smiles.

                    JOHN
          Sounds boring you should dump him.

Mrs. Brooke laughs and kisses John and hugs him tight for
minutes.

                    MRS. BROOKE
          I missed you soo much.

                    JOHN
          I missed you too, I'm so sorry.

                    MRS. BROOKE
          Why did you leave.

                    JOHN
          I was a monster, I was lost and
          those nightmares. I thought I
          didn't belong. I know that was
          wrong.

                    MRS. BROOKE
          This is your family and we love you
          no matter what, you will always
          belong.

John hugs his wife tight.

Kevin smiles and looks at Kristen.

                                        (CONTINUED)

                              KEVIN
                    Wow, alright guys get a room.

                              JOHN
                    Good thinking, how about it Jen?

                              KEVIN
                    Ew, come on now.

                              MRS. BROOKE
                    First things first, you need a
                    bath, because you stink.

Everyone laughs.

                              KEVIN
                    Kristen, this is my father.

                              KRISTEN
                    You look like this homeless guy I
                    know.

John smiles and puts his arm around his wife.

                              JOHN
                    Nah, wasn't me because I have a
                    home, a good home.

John hugs Kevin and his wife.

Kevin grabs Kristen's hand and they walk away from the
parking lot.

32   EXT PARK DAY

Kevin is sitting on the bench with the woman.

The woman is no longer reading her book.

                              KEVIN
                    This piece of paper is that letter
                    from Simon, one year ago today. I
                    guess the moral of the story is
                    Don't judge someone just on their
                    looks or situation and something
                    else I learned that took meeting
                    Simon to understand.

                              WOMAN ON BENCH
                    What's that?

                        KEVIN
          We all have our vices, everyone
          sinks to that low point and needs
          something to pick them up, needless
          to say I see the world differently
          now.

                        WOMAN ON BENCH
          It sounds like you've been through
          quite a lot.

                        KEVIN
          I guess so, I just hope I can help
          people by sharing Simon's story.

The woman gets up and starts to walk but turns back.

                        WOMAN ON BENCH
          Whatever happened to the brother.

                        KEVIN
          We run a business together.

                        WOMAN ON BENCH
          What kind of business.

                        KEVIN
          We run a Medical Marijuana cafe
          called Simon says in Colorado. Part
          of our Profits go to helping those
          effected by prescription drug
          abuse. It's very therapeutic.

                        WOMAN ON BENCH
          Huh, really? would it help my
          anxiety?

                        KEVIN
          Oh we have helped a lot of people
          get over there anxiety, even eating
          disorders. Check us out if you're
          ever in town.

The woman takes a joint out of her purse and takes a hit.

The woman exhales and smiles at Kevin.

                        WOMAN ON BENCH
          Everyone has their vice, I like
          that, you're a fine young man.

                                        (CONTINUED)

                              KEVIN
                    Thank you mam.

The woman smiles and chuckles and walks away.

The woman stops at the homeless man and drops a five dollar
bill in his cup.

                              KEVIN
                    In the end I guess a lot worked
                    out, Simon found peace, I found my
                    father, and Jordan I are helping
                    people. So maybe next time you walk
                    by someone fallen on hard times
                    Don't be an ass because they're
                    people just like you and me. Go out
                    and be a difference. THE END.

As the credits start to roll a couple of junkies walk by.

                              JUNKIE
                    Hey man, you hear about this super
                    oxy?

                              JUNKIE 2
                    Nah man, what is it.

                              JUNKIE
                    Oh man, it's a 160mg the government
                    just released and it's easier to
                    crush and from what I hear more
                    hardcore.

35394409R00057

Made in the USA
Middletown, DE
30 September 2016